Going Out to Gather

Carolyn Adams

Fernwood
PRESS

Going Out to Gather

©2023 by Carolyn Adams

Fernwood Press
Newberg, Oregon
www.fernwoodpress.com

Printed in the United States of America

Cover and interior design: Mareesa Fawver Moss
Cover photo: Annie Spratt

ISBN 978-1-59498-121-0

For the poets, always the poets.

Contents

Acknowledgments

Many thanks to these sources for previously publishing these
poems, some in different versions than presented here:

2010 Poetry at Round Top Anthology: Home Front

2015 Texas Poetry Calendar: 107°

2022 Texas Poetry Calendar: Waking to the Morning

Amsterdam Quarterly: A Frequent Winter Chill

Arlington Literary Journal: Koi Pond

Bayou Review: Shell

Birdsong Journal: Stream Violets

Blueline Magazine: Garter Snake

Bookends Review: Bird, River

Cenizo Journal: Subsistence

Constellate Magazine: Preparing to Bloom

Fleas on the Dog: Rust

Fowl Feathered Review: Moonflower

Fridays on the Boulevard E-zine: Salmon Run

Inverted Syntax: Art of the Postcard: Dawn with arms of roses;
    Tempestuous blue trees

Juxtaprose: Gull on Cobble Beach

Literary Yard: What Spring Also Brings
Manzanita: Poetry & Prose of the Mother Lode & Sierra: Castilleja
Origami Poems Project: NEOWISE
Poetry Post at Multnomah Arts Center, Portland, Oregon: Crow
Poppy Road Review: Multnomah at Night
Radiant Turnstile: Sasulka; Garlands
Riversedge: Cowboy Cemetery; Cicadas
Sequoyah Cherokee River Journal: Now, Morning; Trilliums;
     Turning
Tales from the Trail [YouTube channel]: The Language of Stones
The Weight of Addition: Testament
Tiny Seed Journal: Cannon Beach; This Field Has Eyes, This
     Wood Has Ears
Thrift Poetic Arts Journal: Magnolia, Dying
Untameable City: Poems on the Nature of Houston: Weeds
Willawaw Journal: Going Out to Gather; The Random Notes of
     Autumn
Writers Mill Journal: In Winter's Hush; Map in the Air

The Rust Bells of Winter

In Winter's Hush

I walk a quiet avenue,
the night woven with
deep-throated bells:
a call to worship
or to mourning.
The last of a storm,
its push of fallen leaves
to season's end,
calls me to pursue the hour.
I pass curtained windows,
the laughter of children
and their prayers
against the odd, hulking stranger.
Trees, soon to bud and bloom,
whisper in winter's hush
of another riotous spring.
On broken sidewalks,
I leave the lit path
for outbound streets.

The wind foretells my leaving;
the silence ponders my return.

A Frequent Winter Chill

I'm not from a land of snow.
Where I'm from, you're lucky
to hit freezing twice a year.

I don't know the great loneliness
that sets in, mid-winter,
when the outside is only
a long monotone.

I don't know the struggle of
navigating drifts,
pushing aside boughs
heavy with stones of cold.

Now, in these lovely wilderness valleys,
there's a flurry sometimes
and a frequent winter chill:

when snowflakes fill the woods
with soft ash, when they float
in a tremor of white wings.

Crunching on ice, glad for my boots
on a day like this, I love
the bone-shiver in the air,
the vast silences,
the lace and blades
contouring trees and underbrush.

I love long walks
in the deep alone.

Sasulka

A girl walks these woods
in a dress of broken leaves
and lovely weather,
threaded blue
as the hollows of a snowy day,
brown and russet
as earth-stained water.
Her pale limbs,
her moon-touched shoulders,
slip between the cedars
in their various greens.
Her fingers trail tangled white feathers
in the river.

When the night is clear and cold
and geese row slowly
over the purple sky,
she may whisper at your window
of winter bones and ice on the path,
of solitude and winds gone white.

Leave for her,
in the first snowfall,
what you would rather keep.
Ghosts. Silence.
Love so deep you can't speak of it.
She waits for you.
She listens at the door
for you.

Rust

The rust bells of winter
toll the days in long numbers

as rain, a dark word
on stones,
mantles the air

in heavy garments.
The sun has been absent
for many paragraphs.
My solitude
expands hours

to interminable manuscripts.
I wonder if persistence
can summon heat

from its
abstract origins.
I wonder if
evidentiary storms
can change slight words

to a cogent
argument.
I wonder if
damage truly
alters

what it falls upon.

Koi Pond

The boardwalk,
a treachery of feathers ready
to receive another broken bone,
looms just above the surface.
Step deliberately when approaching.
With few exceptions,
ice has claimed this part of the pond.

This is where you see her,
moving through what
free water remains:
a sluggish ghost in the shadows,
slow, conserving the fragile heat
she still has in this late winter.
A canopy of juniper dressed with light snow
overhangs, watching.

Last year, a quorum of her kind was lost,
turned to stone, to frigid silence.
She doesn't know that story,
but some instinct guides her to keep
what warmth she can, to cruise
in stubborn torpor.

In her drift, she remembers the summer,
her long, languid vowels,
the accompanying texts of her companions.
How they interwove manuscripts,
narrations of sky, tree, sun, and moon.
Warm days are a memory now,
and thoughts rest lightly in her body.

She has held the same posture for an hour.
Her bones have reached a conclusion—
an idea about hope itself—
there, near the indifferent bridge,
inches from the force that will take her.

Waking to the Morning

It's morning on the river.
Reflections line
the shore:
the same wooden fingers
that tap the sky
in gentle recognition
reach from the river
to test their reproduction.
As if there's no difference
between tree and water, air and earth.
As if the slender margins there
could be easily broken
and all the borders of
the world dissolved.

Tundra Swans

Through binoculars, they're improbable.
They don't fit here,
on this reclaimed tributary,
with their humbler cousins—
mallards, gadwalls, wigeons.
Are they slipping through
in some secret migration,
pausing here to feed,
or is this their home ground?
Clarity through the glass
shows their shepherd crooks
held high above the muck
of the marsh, white lace
shirts billowing.
Grace in the shallows,
white foam mirages.
They can't be real.
We don't deserve
their impossibility.

Great Blue Heron

She's a trick of the eye
in the shallows,
motionless.
Breezes lift a feather-frond
from her breast.
For a moment,
you admire her slenderness,
her grace.

But then
she's all dagger and sword.

She lunges.

Her beak stabs the water,
the mud. She eats
a captured minnow,
her eyes a hollow stare.

And you begin to understand
the words: feral, primitive.
The word:
prey.

Gull on Cobble Beach

Have you ever been
a rag on the wind,
forever pursued?

Don't worry that I'm here,
prone, defeated.
I'm glad to rest.

My recessed and rotting eye
watches you lean over me
in sympathy,
afraid to touch
my sodden feathers
or the small,
terrifying red wound
on my breast.
It doesn't hurt me anymore.
Feel my stiff body,
warmed by the sun.
Feel my curled,
retracted-needle feet,
their precise, tiny claws.
Feel my beak,
stripped of what flesh there was,
become naked bone.

Tide Pools

Life swims in basins on the beach,
concavities of old lava left
from the earth's last burning.

When the ocean retreats,
purple urchins and green anemones
fill the sudden shallows.
Kelp, rubbery
as an elephant's ear, flutters
in currents that slip between
pocked stones.

A stranded crab
skitters, finds shelter.
Gulls cruise the exposed shore.
Some small lives will persist
to the next tide; some won't.

The sea hasn't forgotten
these orphan pools.
Foamy arms feel
her way back.

Soon, the moon will bring
the deep water in.

Map in the Air

Gulls and terns cut the wind
with razor wings,
heading west from shore.

I follow
their compass,
their map in the air.

Ten miles out.
Twenty.

We row the sky,
past the shoal
where minnows school,
over that sandbar
where cockles are thick.

I hit the water,
take a fish in my mouth.
I eat
and feel the fish go still.

Its rich salt and flesh
become
my wings, my beak,
my quickened eye.

By Thirty and by Three,
the Spring Days May Come

Preparing to Bloom

I leave you a Lenten rose,
a tender crocus,
in this imaginary spring.

The rain is cold but the sun
teases a change.

We're fooled. We want
to be. But there's more
of winter due;
there's more
revisionary time to come.

For now
I give you these
fleeting colors,
their tender itch just under
the skin—a kind of pain
made small, formed there.

By thirty and by three,
the spring days may come.

Dawn with arms of roses

arrived in plentitude.
Drunk with morning rain,
I was waiting, mouth open
to taste each flower.
Eat its honey. Savor
its velvet. Swallow
the light drowning
in its throat.

(After Sappho)

What Spring Also Brings

They're in a great hurry
in the narrow breeding season.
They don't stop
or pull up short;
they don't correct
their navigation.

The goldfinch against the porch window.
The siskin and the woodpecker at the kitchen glass.
The swift in the flue, on the hearth.

Something clamors
for these deaths.
My house hungers for them.

Their tiny corpse bones haunt.
The silent slender purses of their hearts
close and stop.

Their small soft bodies still.
And still warm.

Magnolia, Dying

She spreads white sheets
like a lover;
she perfumes the bed.
Heavy, waxed petals
thicken in the sun,
drip with honey.
Gold fills her cupped white hand.
But these are her final hours;
this is her only currency.
Soon, her creamy flesh will fade
like the weary light before nightfall.
All that will remain—
a small forgotten need.

Even now
she falters,
in a fading brown dress
and the breath of God.

Weeds

I photograph them
in the mornings,
these precise little flowers
and their microscopic foliage,
growing wild
in the leaf clutter.

They're best in the morning;
too much attention from the sun
and they close up like secrets.

Butter yellow,
salmon pink,
soft lilac,
pale sky blue.

Slipper-shaped.
Five perfect petals,
pin-wheeled.
A bell on a slender stalk.

Assigned such small tasks,
they carry on business almost invisibly.
A shoe tap could destroy them.
Raindrops are catastrophic.

Years ago, I'd mow them
over, pull them out
by roots.
Now I sit with them
in early light
before a clumsy foot
disturbs their industry.

Before it rains.
Before the summer
sends them away.

Shell

The bluest fragment.
A scrap of sky.
The robin
dropped you at my feet,
then looked up expectantly
and fled to the trees.
How could I not
take you with me?

That was a year ago.
I have touched you
many times since then.

Now, the deep fissure
that was just a crack
circles your smooth shoulder.
Your interior has browned;
your blue is dusty, dull.
At your thinnest,
you're almost transparent.

Soon, I won't have you anymore.
You'll crumble
at a tap of my finger.

But I still see you as you were.
I see your mother's eye,
frank and piercing,
giving me responsibility
that very first day.

Garlands

Starlings thread the sky,
their stray loops
picked out, stitched, then unraveled again
from trees and streetlights,
spires and shrubs.
They're everywhere
this time of year,
startling from one promontory to the next.
Black garlands, like tireless applause,
wash the blue stage sky—
a hungry, reckless migration
in constant pursuit.
Suddenly one day,
just when you've come
to expect them,
they're gone,
and the skies are barren and still.

But today
they fill every branch,
every line and rooftop.
Black paper fans,
folding, unfolding,
again and again,
countless restive desires,
countless beating hearts.

Moonflower

I'm walking, sleepless again,
in hours reserved
for criminals and insomniacs like me.
Near a dark window of a shut house,
a white shape floats
with lesser flowers and vines
in the tangle of its moonlit garden.
I lean to cup its fragile face,
to confess some darker truth,
as if it would understand,
being in love with shadows itself.
I don't say what I know,
why I can't turn
to the warm shoulder of sleep,
because I am not yet past that struggle.
It's only a flower, after all,
not meant for that work.
So I leave it
open to the moon and stars,
inclining, as ever,
toward their light.

Bird, River

A bird spills its codes into the air,
resting in the long arms of a tree.

You, stranger bird,
who set you singing
in the secret leaves of coming summer?

It's busy work, stitching the sky to the river.
Some think the job's done
when cloudy stories turn the great wheel
and currents sweep deep disturbances.
But as the river shoulders its way to the sea,
the pattern's still weaving.

Foam is written on the water—
calligraphy, a certain alphabet peculiar to
this river of specificities.

Rain is coming.
Mountains shrug off the horizon.

A branch shudders with its burden.
Eddies swirl in the water.

Now, Morning

I wait as the day shivers open.

(With the wind as company,
a bird and her mate
sing the sun up.)

It will be a long, green time,
and many things will have
taken root—
to flower,
to burst.

This could be the beginning of all things.

I watch a shadow,
like an ill wish,
drape the trees.

It will rain again.
I smell moisture in the air.

There will come a great change.
There is no way to tell
how long this change
has been coming.
There is no way to tell
what the change will be.

All I know is

the temperature's shifted;
the air moves
with a new resolve.

(And the birds
of the earlier hours
have flown.)

Castilleja

You,
thick braids roped down your back,
luminous sienna skin
bearing the heavy heat
of mid-day sun;
you,
lithe in crimson-ochre skirts,
smelling of smoke, leather, sage,
sister to meadowlark and mockingbird,
wild onion, verbena;
you,
daughter of a dreaming earth,
dipped in a florid stain, sunset's fire
for a warrior's temple;
you rise,
unlikely, from dry ground,
undulating
on a windswept prairie,
the air enclosing
your supple grace.

Trilliums

Say
I can sleep with the trilliums tonight.

Say
my husband won't notice my absence, and no one will come
looking.

Say
my enemy won't remember why I'm hated.

Say
the moon will be veiled.

Say
I'm forgiven by their white wings tucked in the forest shadows.
Say their thick stems and broad leaves will hide me. Say I'm
allowed
to witness the morning unfolding of their coiled stamens.

Say
I don't need to explain my hunger for them.

California Poppy

In a field
of endless green,
green-leaved,
poised in a tower of green,
she cups
a bit of yellow.
Quiet gold
in an insufferable sea,
she's hungry
for violet,
indigo,
maybe a touch of crimson.
Sashed
with a blue silk sky,
she waits.
Captive.
Honeyed.
Ready.

Stream Violets

No one planted these little suns.

Untended, they spill artlessly,
inches high, on the forest floor.
Vulnerable to the lightest step,
they drop soft gold
on leaf clutter and dross.

Their yellow tongues
lap pools of light
from small cavities
in the underbrush.

I crouch to touch them,
brush dust from their lips,
turn them up to see me,

knowing there's so much I want
to ask them, so much
I want to say.

Follow, Wait

Slow-rise, temple-high
dawn spills into the valley.
Dream flowers
brush stones
with a lush hand,
covering the passes,
the wet meadows.
Follow the blue river
to the blue sea,
heavy with sky.

Always lost,
this wide window,
to the hum of tires,
spinning pavement,
moving sidewalks.

Wait. Be still.

Now,
stand where you
can find your feet.

Salmon Run

Heavy bodies push
through turgid water, calm water,
rock-heavy water,
only to procreate
and die.

Their devotion tells them
there is nothing else
but this,

to rush through slabs of current,
to eject milky sperm
and jeweled eggs
that will explode into
the fire of life.

Past the dip nets, past the fishers,
past clawing monsters with razor teeth.

Past the sun and the moon.
Past burning sunsets
that mark them crimson.

Past the black velvet sky
and stars,
born and dead
and born again.

When the Summer Moon Rises

The Language of Stones

Listen to what this place tells you.
The story is long.
Words can't substitute for water,
but the air itself carries power.
It could feed you.

You may walk long miles
with only the language of stones
to accompany you.
Joshua trees and scrub
stand in this broad open, dry to the touch
but alive. You can hardly believe
there is life around you.

A sere palette in drought gradations
brushes the ground underfoot.
Dun, rust, copper, gold.
What survives and what doesn't
leave their marks nonetheless.

Top a low ridge, in a direction
you didn't intend, and the desert sings
a sudden song of crimson.
The burden you carry lightens.
Short leaf crimson
spreads the ground, fills crevices.
Crimson over stones,
crimson over sand,
crimson under brush.

And you begin to sense life
where you thought it was lost.
A tiny reptile, skittering.
A bird returning to its nest.
An animal, small and unnamed,
behind a stone, watching.
Then you hear a low hum
of joy and tenderness,
a desert song in a new language.
A song of remembered history.
A song of light and living.
And you begin
to sing along.

Cowboy Cemetery

Weathered barns gleam
in clean, dry heat;
the wisp of hawk wings
glides an azure sky.
Mesquite tempts a search for shade
under tough green tendrils;
cedar greedily siphons weary ground.
Cemetery trees guard a plot of land
hewn from bedrock,
as a gate creaks on rusted hinges
drilled into thick limestone walls.
Where scorpions lift delicate barbs
above armored backs
to skitter over stones and scrub weeds,
engraved marble headstones recite lineages,
and crude sandstone shards mumble simple farewells.
A restive wind sweeps valleys
and rocky slopes,
hurries a day's ride to the east
and north to town.

107°

Stay in the shade
and you won't notice it.
Or maybe
it won't notice you.

Watch the shifting patterns
of clouds on the ground.
The precarious departure
of birds from their nests.
Their fragile wings.

Feel the gradations
of the air.

Once, I learned
an old lesson:
let the worst,
with its intricate tasks,
become the hardest thing
in your body.
Soften around it.

You'll sense
what you've taken for granted.

The pulse
in your temples,
the fine wires of nerves
in your fingertips.

The myriad sounds
collapsing
around you.

Home Front

Hawks, those B-52s of the bird world,
reconnoiter a nearby pasture.

>Black-eyed Susans stare them down.
>The dandelions, little Dorothys,
>primp in the sun.

They cruise a blue sky-plain,
both barrels cocked.

>Winecups, drunk on their own
>Tallulah Bankhead impressions,
>ally with the enemy.

They close in.
Nothing in the field is asking why.
Every living thing knows.

>The Johnson grass quietly grieves,
>its seed-heads beating the hay bales
>at the meadow's edge.

But the hawks only pass over,
shadows rippling,
ruffling weeds,
the trigger, for now, on safety.

Cicadas

Cicadas rev their green machines
in twilight,
even in the dark
when the summer moon rises.

"Heat overpasses us,"
they hum,
"and earth is only earth."

Those winged rowers steam into
the night, keep the treetop presses
rolling through dawn.

Geese

Their scat scents a field of summer
long after they've moved on.

Feathers among the moth mullein, old droppings
in the brown grass where the tansy blooms.

A female rested here. The flock lingered near the pond.

Periscope sentinels guarded the perimeter—
black heads, black pearl eyes, at high alert.
The others browsed and fed.
A trail was worn to the water.

You can almost hear them in overflight.
Calls echoing in the meadows,
multiples of a single note that's many, unified.

In six weeks, they'll return.

They weigh so heavy in your memory,
it's as if they never left.

Multnomah at Night

From downstream
a cold push, a rush.
Continents of water
displacing.

Grandmother bones
of basalt hold it back
only by inches,
funneling its thunder.

The night clock moves
as ever in the presence
of this power.

Some animals manage sleep
nearby; others stir
in their hunting hours.

Ferns uphold
poised swords;
lichens cling to
protective stones.

In that cathedral grotto,
the dark crescendos
must be unbearable.

Tempestuous blue trees

stretch from horizon
to horizon.
It's such a beautiful day.
Can you reach up
to the highest limbs,
pull them down to
this undeserving earth?
I'll climb with you,
tame the blue heights,
push aside the sun,
and look into
the faces of stars.
We'll be light-struck,
storm-tossed.

I Left and Walked Up into the Air

It was easy,
wearing clouds for shoes.
With each footfall
there was a summer shower,
and when I stomped
there was a gust.
Looking down on everything,
I was weightless.
And the atmosphere
was like a wet garden
when the sun has risen
and the whole of the day
stretches out before you,
naked,
new.

NEOWISE

In last night's wandering hours,
with the transient moon loose
in another hemisphere,

you broke in the Northwest—
a fire stick
dodging the Big Dipper.

You paused,
almost frozen.
It was a trick of the eye:
with me going one way and
you another, we met

in sympathetic arcs.
I wanted to capture you,
but you were leaving.

You fought your way
to somewhere else,
at the whim of some planet or sun.
It's six thousand years

before you're here again.
Of course, we're all dead by then.
An ancestor
may watch your ball of ice

shoot the deep darkness
and fear, finally,
the millennia
in your devil tail dress.

blue dot **sky blue** **night blue**

blue light	too blue	far blue
water blue	cool blue	soft blue
blue home	space blue	dream blue

Cannon Beach

Volcanic blue
advances.
Salt lace tatters
the hair
of a wakening giant.
Twig birds
pick the shallows,
glassy sand melting
under their feet.
The beach braces
as the sea
throws all
its crystal chandeliers
at once.

I could take a thousand pictures

of her.
What lives there
clocks to the rhythm
of what never changes.

I can see it now,
that blue Pacific beast
in the early morning,
sun-burnished.

And again,
in the dark,
echoing rings
of the moon's
cool light.

It's a long song.
It's a continued
conversation.

The Random Notes of Autumn

Going Out to Gather

Sunlight doesn't reach the ground.
The foliage folds around me,
and I am going out to gather.
There are animals and birds here,
tiny flowers of bindweed and wild radish,
cones the size of my fingertip.
I am walking out in all of this;
I am going out alone.

I pull my coat close.

It's dry, but the evergreens
remember rain.
Maples are green going gold,
gold going red, red burning to rust.
Moss and lichen revise bark and limb.
A crow cruises and watches as I watch her.
She drops a feather.

My fingers curl over my pocketed key.

I am going out to gather;
I am walking out in all of this.
Small animals crush quietly
the leaves and twigs in dark underbrush.
A breeze hushes the tops of the trees.
Sedge flows with the wind.

In a clearing is a swath of unfamiliar light.
The ground is ash, charcoal splinters.
Trees and launches of skeletal berry vines
are charred ghosts.
Someone has been here before me.
The air is acrid with smoke memory.

I release a breath.

Nothing will be kept but the crow feather,
the cone, the moss.
I am going out to gather.
I am walking out alone.

Garter Snake

She cruises the deep recesses
of the underbrush,
surfacing
to crest weed stubble,
then slipping low
between tall,
dry stalks.

Sometimes, she ponders
the cool light of the season.
Her frank eye neither accepts
nor rejects
the presence of anything.

Her armor is so green
it's black.
Her torso
that is her body entire
is studded with orange rubies,
a sinuous green sash.
She knows
she is beautiful.
She extends a rough-muscled tongue
to taste the air,
a split-ribbon antenna,
gauging
the presence of things.

Then she resumes
her circuitous
weaving,
taking into account
obstacles and threats.

Her progress
is not an argument,
exactly.

Crow

One tenacious crow
in the fire maple,
calling, holding
to her one song,
its two notes,
the upper and lower registers
of the same color.

She declares:
This is mine. Mine alone.
This tree, this earth,
this convex sky.
She stamps her claim
on every listening ear.

Her tenacity
could be mistaken
for conceit.

Others try
from a distance—
robins, sparrows, doves.
Their waverings
ripple harmlessly
into the atmosphere.
They're stumblers.

She knows
what she's made for.
She knows
what's hers.

Subsistence

Witness
an act ancient and absolute:
a hawk subdues
a clumsy, lesser bird.
Beak, talon,
unflinching will.

Feeding
on her mantled prey
in the fallen leaves,
the hawk is in no hurry.

Resting, working.
Shredding useful flesh.

The air, restive,
seeks another tableau.

The light holds,
waiting for her
to rise,
to recede again
into the hell
of her origin.

Nutria

Snuffle-faced,
whiskered,
a nightmare mermaid
slumps from the marsh,
oily,
feral.

You recoil.

Given the chance,
she'll slip
into your house, bite
your leg, soil your
best sheets.
She won't be welcome.

What do you expect
from a surrogate
sacrifice, body-double
for the fur trade
of a hundred
years ago.

She didn't ask for this.

She stares at you
for a moment,
then shambles back into
the muddy water,
shoulders herself
away from you,

flips her scaly
rat tail to splash
at you as she
swims to the
culvert.

Testament

Within a stand of tall cedars,
a doe fell prey in early spring,

her panicked eye reflecting white
from a predatory moon.

The ground shifted beneath her feet
then settled back to what it was,

her falling body fitted to
the hollows of the wooded field.

She lies there still, her tattered pelt
now emptied by the scavengers

who kept their watch and cleaned each bone
of all its necessary flesh.

As the southern constellations
sweep light and dust in equal measure,

the grass sings in a testament
to all the turning earth provides.

The night birds leave their nesting trees
to fold into the autumn dark

and take their places in the sky
against another hungry moon.

The Random Notes of Autumn

These are the random notes of autumn.

The lostness of birds left behind
when migration ends.
The crash of a young creature
in the underbrush.
A late honeybee's wandering stitches.
Persistent crickets in secret leaves.
The miracle of a single acorn falling,
its small wood
still warm,
still remembering its tree.

Turning

The ponds this time of year
are cool and clear.
The reeds ringing them,
brown and waiting,
rest easy in the season.

The sun turns a shoulder
to the fields, casting its eye
obliquely. Revising its stance.
Taking another look
at what it thinks the landscape
should resemble.

Search for a little green
and you might find the bindweed
still blooming, still turning
their white-pink thimbles
to the gentle light.

And reaching out from
the fallow brush, willow sticks
with cat's toes up and down
their stems. Silver fur tufted
soft as any fine hairs
on any fine cat
prowling its way through
these meadows,
sidling its way home.

Mist in Evergreens

Mist diminishes the evergreens,
hiding laden branches,
shifting trunks, melding them
with fog shadows.

The forest becomes a small room.

Rain taps the shoulders
of the trees, reminding them
they need water.

From a low branch, a mat of lichen falls,
damp and soft,
still holding its concavity.

The shower passes.
The woods are cooled, clean.
Windows of air
clarify the silence.

Geese navigate the treetops,
heading south,
folding the sky
at its seams.

This Field Has Eyes, This Wood Has Ears

In the canopy,
on the floor,
a story is written
on stem, tangle-vine,
and rock.

Owl sits in judgment.
Raven disputes the verdict.
Field mouse musters
a new defense.

Elms drape greenwood
with brown rag leaves,
discarded, derelict.
A delicate worry.

In a small clearing,
a mat of feathers,
soft and gray as the overcast sky,
cradles delicate bones in
a white we all know.
They slowly crumble into
the dust we also know.

This is the circle we're in,
its ebbs and flows.
This is the beautiful, awful language
of this life.

Author Biography

Carolyn Adams, originally from Houston, Texas, has lived in Beaverton, Oregon, since 2017. From childhood, her passion has been reading and writing poetry, and as an adult, she has cultivated a love of photography and art. While living in Houston, she was active in the art and literary communities of Houston, Austin, and other parts of Texas for many years, coordinating and performing in numerous readings, festivals, literary events, and art exhibitions. In 2013, she was a finalist for Houston Poet Laureate. She received her undergraduate degree in Humanities from the University of Houston in 2016. She has been nominated for a Pushcart prize and for Best of the Net. Since her move to Oregon, she has connected with poets in her new home and continues her involvement in the local scene, as well as taking frequent trips into the beautiful natural environment of her new home state. Her poetry, art, and photography have appeared in *Caveat Lector, Steam Ticket, Bryant Literary Review, The Weight of Addition: An Anthology of Texas Poetry, Common Ground Review, Beatnik Cowboy, Kansas City*

Voices, *San Pedro River Review*, and *Cimarron Review*, among others. She has assisted in editing and publishing the literary journals *Curbside Review*, *Ardent*, *Lily Literary Review*, *Mad Hatters Review*, *Mojave River Review* and *VoiceCatcher*. Her poetry e-chapbook *Beautiful Strangers* was published in 2006 by Lily Press, and her art e-chapbook, *What Do you See?*, published in 2007, is available free of charge from the e-zine *Right Hand Pointing*. She has also published two chapbooks, *An Ocean of Names* in 2011, and *The Things You've Left Behind* in 2016.

Title Index

First Line Index

H

I

L

M

N

O

9 781594 981210